InnerNex

Navigating Feelings on the Page

Table of Contents

CHAPTER 1 INTRODUCTION:

- The Importance of Emotional Intelligence
- How Fiction Reflects Real Emotions
- Purpose of the Book

CHAPTER 2 BASICS OF EMOTIONS:

- Definitions
- The Range of Human Emotions
- Physical vs. Psychological Responses

CHAPTER 3 THE PAGE EMOTION SPOTLIGHTS:

➲ Individual Emotions Including - Happiness, Love, Surprise

CHAPTER 4 EMOTION RELATES:

- Analyzing Emotions in Fiction w/Practical Exercises
- Character Emotional Journey

CHAPTER 5 EMOTIONAL THEMES AND ARCHETYPES IN FICTION:

➲ Identifying Emotions in Fiction

CHAPTER 6 EMOTION ANALYSIS IN ACTION BY EXAMPLES:

➲ Applying InnerNex Techniques in Real Life Challenges

➲ Identifying Emotions: Fiction vs. Reality

CHAPTER 7 EMOTION IDENTIFICATION SKILLS:

➡ Blind Read

➡ Character Emotional Journaling

➡ Emotion Mapping and More

CHAPTER 8 INTERPRETING EMOTIONAL SIGNALS IN FICTION:

➥Unlocking Subtext Submarines

CHAPTER 9 FICTION ANALYSIS:

➲ Habits Practiced Hone Skill

CHAPTER 10 EMOTION EXERCISES AND PRACTICE SCENARIOS:

➲ Sample Scenarios for Emotion Opening

➲ Solutions and Breakdowns

CHAPTER 11 ADVANCED INNERNEX TECHNIQUES AND TIPS:

- ➲ Advanced Methods for Unlocking Emotions
- ➲ Handling Ambiguous Emotional Signals

CHAPTER 12 INNERNEX IN MODERN MEDIA:

- ➲ Analyzing Emotions in Movies, TV Shows, and More
- ➲ InnerNex's Relevance in Digital Media

CHAPTER 13 REAL-LIFE APPLICATION:

- Enhancing Empathy and Social Skills
- The Everyday Impact of InnerNex

CHAPTER 14 YOUR INNER JOURNEY:

- Application
- Engaging Activities to Hone Skills
- Scenario-based Practice Sessions

CHAPTER 15 INNERNEX APPLICATION:

- ➲ Diverse Applications of InnerNex
- ➲ Challenges and Triumphs

CHAPTER 16 LIFE IN ACTION:

- ➲ InnerNex's Role in Real-life Interactions
- ➲ Real Life's Emotional Twists

CHAPTER 17 ADVANCED TECHNIQUES AND CHALLENGES IN INNERNEX APPLICATION:

⭢ Advanced Scenarios and Challenges

CHAPTER 18 INNERNEX IN DIFFERENT LITERARY GENRES:

➲ Applying InnerNex Across Genres

➲ Genre-specific Emotional Cues

CHAPTER 19 EMOTIONS BEYOND WORDS:

➲ Interpreting Silent Moments in Fiction

➲ Reading Between the Lines

CHAPTER 20 CONNECTING WITH CHARACTERS: THE INNERNEX WAY:

- Deepening Emotional Connections with Fictional Characters
- The Role of InnerNex in Relatability

CHAPTER 21 CHALLENGES AND SOLUTIONS:

➲ Overcoming InnerNex Hurdles

➲ Tips for Tricky Scenarios

CHAPTER 22 APPLIED INNERNEX: REAL-WORLD SCENARIOS:

CHAPTER 23 EXAMPLES & EXERCISES:

➲ Practical InnerNex Applications

➲ Exercises with Solutions

CHAPTER 24 APPLICATIONS BEYOND FICTION:

- ➲ InnerNex in Daily Life
- ➲ InnerNex in Media and Popular Culture

CHAPTER 25 USING INNERNEX TO PREDICT CHARACTER ACTIONS:

●Predictive Analysis Using InnerNex

●Reading Ahead in Fiction

CHAPTER 26 DECIPHERING COMPLEX EMOTIONS WITH INNERNEX:

➲ Handling Mixed Emotions
➲ Depth Analysis Techniques

CHAPTER 27 INNERNEX IN PLAY:

● Growth The Best Way

● Engaging Activities for Skill Enhancement

CHAPTER 28 EMO-TUNING YOUR INNERNEX SKILLS:

●Broader Context Techniques

CHAPTER 29 ADDING ANOTHER ANGLE:

➲ Additional Applications

CHAPTER 30 APPLYING INNERNEX IN DAILY LIFE:

CHAPTER 33 CLOSING THOUGHTS AND FURTHER EXPLORATION:

➲ Reflecting on the InnerNex Journey

➲ Future Prospects and Applications

CH. 1 INTRODUCTION:

Emotions are the heartbeats of stories. They breathe life into characters, give depth to narratives, and connect readers to fictional worlds. Recognizing a character's sadness, anger, or elation is one aspect; truly understanding the intricate web of emotions from textual cues is another.

In InnerNex, we'll explore the art of discerning emotions in fictional scenarios. This easy digest guide is not just about deepening your reading experience but also about refining your ability to perceive and understand emotions in various contexts.

As you journey through this easy digest guide, you'll delve into the myriad hues of emotions, from the overt to the beautifully subtle, complemented by lighthearted detours along the way.

Emotional intelligence, often abbreviated as EI or EQ (Emotional Quotient), stands as a cornerstone in our ability to navigate the complexities of interpersonal relationships. It transcends beyond mere recognition of emotions, encapsulating our capacity to manage, harness, and respond to these feelings, both in ourselves and in others.

1. Enhancing Interpersonal Relationships:
Humans are inherently social beings. Our ability to form and maintain relationships—whether familial, friendly, or romantic—is crucial to our well-being. A heightened emotional intelligence allows us to comprehend the emotional landscapes of those around us, fostering empathy, understanding, and deeper connections.

2. Effective Decision Making:
Contrary to the popular belief that decisions should be purely rational, emotions invariably influence our choices. Recognizing and understanding these emotions ensures that we make decisions that are not just logical, but also emotionally sound.

3. Self-awareness and Personal Growth:
Emotional intelligence paves the way for introspection. By recognizing and understanding our emotional responses, we can reflect upon our actions, habits, and behaviors, leading to personal growth and self-improvement.

4. Conflict Resolution:
Disagreements and conflicts are inevitable in our interactions. A person equipped with a high

EQ can discern the emotions at play, allowing for effective communication, understanding the root causes, and fostering resolutions that cater to all parties involved.

5. Adaptability in Changing Environments:
Our world is in a state of constant flux, and change is an ever-present factor in our lives. Emotional intelligence aids in recognizing the emotional upheavals that come with change, ensuring we adapt smoothly and maintain our mental well-being.

In the realm of fiction, characters display a spectrum of emotional intelligence, from those who are deeply attuned to the feelings of others to those who struggle with emotional recognition. As readers, when we enhance our own emotional intelligence, it allows us to connect more deeply with these characters, understanding their motives, actions, and inner worlds. But beyond the pages, honing our EI serves us in the grander narrative of life, enriching our experiences and interactions.

The world of fiction often appears to be a realm of imagination, a space where boundaries blur, and anything is possible. Yet, at its core, fiction derives its power from a profound truth: its ability to mirror, magnify, and delve into the very emotions that define our human experience.

1. Universal Emotional Themes:
From ancient epics to modern novels, stories from different cultures and epochs seem to converge on universal emotional themes. Love, betrayal, ambition, fear, and hope are but a few. These emotions are as palpable in the poetic laments of Greek tragedies as they are in contemporary dystopian novels.

2. Characters as Emotional Vessels:
Characters in fiction are meticulously crafted emotional vessels. Through them, authors channel a spectrum of feelings, creating relatable beings. When a character rejoices, mourns, or rages, we, as readers, resonate with them, seeing fragments of our own emotional journeys reflected in their tales.

3. Fictional Scenarios, Authentic Reactions:
Even in the most fantastical or otherworldly settings, characters' emotional responses are rooted in authentic human reactions. A dragon might be a mythical creature, but the fear it instills in a village, or the awe it evokes in a protagonist, mirrors genuine human emotions we might feel in face of real-life challenges or wonders.

4. Amplification and Exploration:
Fiction often amplifies emotions, taking them to their zenith or nadir, allowing readers to explore the depths and heights of feeling. This heightened emotional landscape helps us confront and understand our own emotions, even those we might suppress or shy away from in daily life.

5. Emotional Evolution:
Just as we evolve and grow emotionally through our life experiences, characters in fiction undergo emotional arcs. Witnessing these arcs—be it redemption, descent into chaos, or personal growth—provides insights into the resilience and malleability of the human spirit.

6. Empathy and Perspective:
Diverse narratives give readers a window into lives, cultures, and experiences far removed from their own. This broadens our emotional horizons, cultivating empathy, understanding, and a more inclusive perspective.

In essence, fiction acts as a mirror to our souls. It does not just portray emotions; it beckons us to feel, introspect, and connect. By understanding emotions in fiction, we gain a richer appreciation for the tapestry of feelings that color our reality.

The intricate dance of words on a page can stir the heart, inspire the mind, and evoke a kaleidoscope of emotions. Yet, the delicate nuances of these emotions, especially in fictional scenarios, can often elude even the most seasoned reader. This is where "InnerNex" steps in.

1. Deepen Emotional Understanding:
Unravel the layers of emotions portrayed in fiction. It is designed not merely to identify but to truly understand the subtleties, triggers, and manifestations of various feelings, elevating the reader's emotional acuity.

2. Bridge Fiction and Reality:
The primary lens is focused on fictional scenarios, the emotional insights gleaned are universally applicable. Through "InnerNex," readers will not only become adept at discerning fictional emotions but also at recognizing and empathizing with real-world feelings, both in themselves and others.

3. Equip Educators and Enthusiasts:
For educators, readers, therapists this book is offering tools and techniques to discuss, analyze, and teach the emotional dimensions of literary works.

4. Enrich Reading Experience:
By understanding the emotional underpinnings of characters and narratives, readers can immerse themselves deeper into the story. This book endeavors to amplify the reading experience, making each page more vivid, relatable, and impactful.

5. Promote Emotional Intelligence:
Drawing parallels between fictional and real emotions, this guide also doubles as a resource to enhance one's emotional intelligence. It underscores the importance of emotional awareness in personal development and interpersonal relationships.

6. Celebrate the Art of Storytelling:
At its heart, InnerNex is also a tribute to the timeless art of storytelling. By exploring emotions in fiction, we are celebrating the power of stories to reflect, shape, and transcend human experience.

The aspiration is that if even a few insights resonate or a moment of clarity is achieved, the journey within these pages would be considered valuable. The beauty often lies in deepening one's understanding of even a single emotion, as it can significantly enrich interactions and introspection.

CH. 2 BASICS OF EMOTIONS:

1. What are Emotions?
At the most fundamental level, emotions are reactions to internal and external events. They can arise from thoughts, memories, external stimuli, or interactions, and they influence our thoughts, behaviors, and physiological states leading to physiological reactions in our bodies.

2. The Difference Between Emotions and Feelings:
Though often used interchangeably, emotions and feelings are distinct. Emotions are immediate, automatic responses to stimuli. Feelings, on the other hand, are the conscious experiences and interpretations of those emotions over time.

3. Primary Emotions:
Primary or basic emotions are universal and biologically driven. Examples include happiness, sadness, fear, anger, surprise, and disgust. These are experienced similarly across cultures and even species.

4. Complex Emotions:
Derived from primary emotions, complex emotions are multifaceted and often culturally or situationally specific. Examples include jealousy, pride, shame, and nostalgia.

5. The Physiological Aspect:
Every emotion has a corresponding physiological response. Fear might quicken the heart rate, while sadness might lead to a drop in energy. Understanding this link is crucial as it emphasizes that emotions are not just mental experiences but holistic body reactions.

6. Emotions and Cognition:
Our thought processes influence and are influenced by our emotions. For instance, positive emotions can foster creativity, while negative emotions might narrow our focus.

7. Emotional Regulation:
It's the ability to manage and modify emotional responses. Emotional regulation skills can enhance well-being, improve relationships, and promote mental health.

8. The Lifespan of an Emotion:
An emotion doesn't last forever. It arises, peaks, and subsides. Recognizing the transient nature of emotions can aid in coping and understanding.

9. Emotions and Communication:
Emotions serve as a primary form of non-verbal communication. From the arch of an eyebrow to the curve of the lips, emotions convey messages more potent than words.

10. The Role of Emotions in Decision Making:
Contrary to the notion of cold, calculated decisions, emotions play a significant role in our choices, often acting as shortcuts to drive rapid responses.

Emotions, in their depth and complexity, form the cornerstone of human experience. Drawing on foundational concepts found in works such as Goleman's "Emotional Intelligence" and Johnston's exploration of the science behind emotions, present key terminologies to better understand this intricate realm:

1. Emotion:
A complex psychological state involving a range of physiological and cognitive responses to a stimulus or situation. Emotions are often brief but powerful, and, as Goleman highlights, they play an integral role in human intelligence and decision-making processes.

2. Feeling:
The subjective experience of an emotion. This differentiation between emotion and feeling aided by Johnston's exploration of the evolutionary reasons for these experiences, emphasizing the conscious awareness of our automatic emotional reactions.

3. Mood:
Lasting longer than feelings or emotions, moods set the general tone of our emotional state. They are like the background music to our daily emotional experiences.

4. Affect:
The observable manifestation of emotions, be it through facial expressions, body language, or tone of voice. This external presentation is our way of communicating our inner emotional state to the world.

5. Temperament:
An individual's consistent pattern of emotional reactions. Deeply rooted in both genetics and early experiences, temperament shapes our default emotional setting.

6. Emotional Intelligence (EI):
As introduced by Goleman, EI entails recognizing, managing, and effectively expressing one's emotions while understanding and navigating those of others. High EI is indicative of adept social interactions and relationships.

7. Empathy:
The capacity to understand another's emotions and experiences. While Goleman discusses

the value of empathy in interpersonal skills, it's crucial to distinguish it from the next term.

8. Sympathy:
Feelings of compassion for someone else's situation. Unlike empathy, it doesn't necessarily involve understanding or sharing the emotional experience.

9. Emotional Resonance:
When emotions in one person evoke similar emotions in another. It's the mutual understanding or connection felt during deep emotional interactions.

10. Catharsis:

The act of releasing suppressed emotions. This concept is explored in various psychological works, pointing towards the healing and renewing power of expressing and confronting our emotions, be it through art, conversation, or introspection.

Emotions, though universally experienced, are vast in their spectrum.

1. Primary Emotions:
These are innate emotions experienced universally across cultures. They are immediate responses to stimuli, often without much cognitive processing.

- Joy: An uplifting emotion, often accompanied by sensations of lightness and an increase in energy.

- Sadness: A feeling of sorrow or unhappiness, often stemming from loss or disappointment.

- Fear: An anticipatory emotion in response to potential threats or dangers.

- Disgust: A strong aversion to something perceived as unpleasant or offensive.

- Anger: A response to perceived injustice or threats to oneself or loved ones.

- Surprise: A sudden emotion in response to an unexpected event or situation.

2. Secondary Emotions:
Derived from primary emotions, they're more nuanced and can be culturally influenced.

- Pride: A positive emotion that results from a personal achievement or the recognition of one's values.

- Jealousy: A protective or wary feeling related to a perceived threat to a valued relationship or to one's self-esteem.

- Shame: A feeling of humiliation or distress caused by consciousness of wrong or foolish behavior.

➲ Guilt: Often arises from a perceived wrongdoing, whether real or imagined.

➲ Envy: A feeling of discontented or resentful longing aroused by someone else's possessions, qualities, or luck.

3. Complex Emotions:

These emotions often involve intricate blends of primary and secondary emotions, and they can evolve over time, often influenced by introspection, external feedback, and personal experiences.

➲ Euphoria: Intense excitement and happiness, often surpassing the simplicity of joy.

➲ Melancholy: A reflective sadness about life's experiences or an undefined yearning.

➲ Ambivalence: Simultaneous and contradictory feelings or attitudes toward an object, person, or action.

➲ Nostalgia: A sentimental longing for the past, typically for a period or place with happy associations.

4. Emotional Combinations:

There are moments when multiple emotions coexist, leading to a unique emotional experience.

➲ Bittersweet: Feeling happy and sad at the same time, often when saying goodbye to a loved one or reflecting on past memories.

➲ Anxious Excitement: A mix of anticipation and nervousness about an upcoming event or situation.

Recognizing the vast range of emotions helps in understanding human behavior better. It's crucial to note that emotions aren't static; they flow and evolve, shaped by personal experiences, cultural influences, and even biological factors. By understanding and acknowledging these varied emotions, one fosters a deeper connection with oneself and others.

to discern the differences between physical and psychological responses. Emotions manifest in both domains, but the distinction between the two can sometimes be blurry. Let's dissect these intertwined facets of emotional reactions.

1. The Physical Side of Emotions

Emotions, in many instances, trigger physiological responses. Fear might make our hearts race, while sadness can manifest in tears.

⮕ Automatic Responses: Our body has a built-in system, primarily controlled by the autonomic nervous system, that responds to emotional stimuli. These are often instantaneous and uncontrollable, like the dilation of pupils in response to surprise.

⮕ Chemical Reactions: Emotions release different chemicals and hormones. For instance, happiness often releases serotonin and dopamine, while stress prompts the release of cortisol.

2. The Psychological Side of Emotions

While our bodies might react physically to emotions, the mind interprets, labels, and often intensifies these emotions.

⮕ Cognitive Appraisal: Before we even recognize an emotion, our mind has already interpreted a situation. This cognitive process can shape the intensity and type of emotion we experience.

⮕ Emotional Memory: Our past experiences, traumas, and joys all shape how we psychologically respond to current emotions. An event that's insignificant to one might be deeply traumatic for another because of their emotional memories.

3. The Interconnection

⮕ Feedback Loops: Physical responses can amplify psychological ones and vice versa. For instance, noticing our rapid heartbeat (physical) can escalate our feelings of anxiety (psychological).

⮕ Cultural & Social Impacts: Physical expressions of emotions (like crying) can be influenced by psychological conditioning. In some cultures, public displays of certain emotions might be suppressed or exaggerated because of societal norms.

4. InnerNex's Approach

InnerNex doesn't merely label an emotion; it delves into the intricacies of both physical and psychological responses. By understanding the depth of emotional reactions, InnerNex provides a more comprehensive emotional profile.

⮕ Quantifying Physical Responses: InnerNex provides tools and methods to measure and interpret various physiological responses linked to emotions, ensuring an objective representation.

⮕ Interpreting Psychological Reactions: Using cognitive analysis techniques and personal emotional history, InnerNex aids in understanding the psychological facet of emotions.

Physical and psychological responses to emotions are two sides of the same coin. By understanding and distinguishing between them, InnerNex offers a holistic view of human emotional responses. Recognizing these intertwined facets equips us with the ability to better comprehend, communicate, and manage our emotional well-being.

CH. 3 THE PAGE EMOTION SPOTLIGHTS:

1. Happiness

> ➲ A state of well-being and contentment, often accompanied by feelings of joy or pleasure.

> ➲ Fictional Triggers and Manifestations: Winning a lottery; a child's laughter; receiving praise for a job well done.

> ➲ Textual Scenarios and Examples: Sarah felt a surge of happiness as she watched her daughter take her first steps.

> ➲ Common Misreads and Misunderstandings: Over-exuberance can sometimes be mistaken for insincerity or sarcasm.

2. Sadness

> ➲ An emotional state characterized by feelings of disappointment, loss, or helplessness.

> ➲ Fictional Triggers and Manifestations: Losing a beloved pet; failing an important test; recalling painful memories.

> ➲ Textual Scenarios and Examples: David felt an overwhelming sadness when he remembered the holidays with his late grandmother.

> ➲ Common Misreads and Misunderstandings: Sadness can sometimes be interpreted as disinterest or aloofness.

3. Anger

> ➲ A strong feeling of displeasure and antagonism, often arising from a perceived wrong or injustice.

> ➲ Fictional Triggers and Manifestations: Being falsely accused; witnessing an act of cruelty; being cut off in traffic.

➲ Textual Scenarios and Examples: Claire's anger bubbled up when she realized her colleague had taken credit for her work.

➲ Common Misreads and Misunderstandings: Passion or intensity can sometimes be mistaken for anger.

4. Fear

➲ An unpleasant emotion caused by the belief that someone or something is dangerous or a threat.

➲ Fictional Triggers and Manifestations: Walking alone in a dark alley; hearing an unexpected noise at night; facing an aggressive animal.

➲ Textual Scenarios and Examples: Tim's heart raced with fear when he noticed the shadowy figure following him.

➲ Common Misreads and Misunderstandings: Caution or wariness can sometimes be mistaken for fear.

5. Surprise

➲ An unexpected event or piece of information that causes astonishment or disbelief.

➲ Fictional Triggers and Manifestations: A surprise birthday party; an unexpected gift; hearing unexpected news.

➲ Textual Scenarios and Examples: Anna gasped in surprise when her friends yelled, "Happy Birthday!" from behind the curtains.

➲ Common Misreads and Misunderstandings: Surprise can sometimes be interpreted as shock or fear, especially if the individual is taken off guard.

6. Disgust

➲ A strong revulsion or aversion towards something perceived as unpleasant or offensive.

➲ Fictional Triggers and Manifestations: Encountering rotten food; witnessing an act of cruelty; inappropriate behaviors.

➲ Textual Scenarios and Examples: Mike's face wrinkled in disgust when he saw the trash littering the beautiful beach.

➲ Common Misreads and Misunderstandings: Strong dislike or distaste can sometimes be mistaken for disgust.

7. Jealousy

⮞An emotional response stemming from envy of someone else's possessions, qualities, or good fortune, often coupled with a fear of losing something or someone of great personal importance.

⮞Fictional Triggers and Manifestations: Seeing a friend's success overshadowing your own; a partner's close relationship with a coworker; someone else receiving praise for a similar accomplishment.

⮞Textual Scenarios and Examples: Lisa's heart sank with jealousy when she saw how everyone admired Maria's new artwork.

⮞Common Misreads and Misunderstandings: Jealousy can sometimes be misinterpreted as simple sadness or anger without understanding the underlying envy.

8. Anticipation

⮞The emotion involving pleasure, excitement, and sometimes anxiety in considering or awaiting an expected event.

⮞Fictional Triggers and Manifestations: Waiting for the results of an exam; the moments before a surprise is revealed; awaiting a loved one's return.

⮞Textual Scenarios and Examples: Mark's anticipation grew as the countdown to the rocket launch began.

⮞Common Misreads and Misunderstandings: Anticipation can sometimes be misinterpreted as impatience or anxiety.

9. Love

⮞An intense and deep affection, attraction, and care for someone or something. It is a complex set of emotions, behaviors, beliefs, and values.

⮞Fictional Triggers and Manifestations: A couple's intimate moments; a parent's care for their child; the bond between close friends.

⮞Textual Scenarios and Examples: Every time Naomi looked into Paul's eyes, she felt an overwhelming sense of love.

⮞Common Misreads and Misunderstandings: Deep friendship or admiration can sometimes be mistaken for romantic love. Similarly, infatuation can be misinterpreted as genuine love.

10. Enthusiasm

○A feeling of lively interest and eagerness in relation to a particular subject or activity.

○Fictional Triggers and Manifestations: Embarking on a new project; engaging in a favorite hobby; attending a highly anticipated event.

○Textual Scenarios and Examples: Alex's enthusiasm was palpable as he outlined his vision for the community project.

○Common Misreads and Misunderstandings: Overzealousness can sometimes be viewed as insincerity or as trying too hard.

11. Despair

○A feeling of utter loss of hope or a lack of belief in positive outcomes.

○Fictional Triggers and Manifestations: Experiencing repeated failures; facing insurmountable challenges; enduring prolonged isolation.

○Textual Scenarios and Examples: After the third failed attempt to save the family business, Oliver sank into a pit of despair.

○Common Misreads and Misunderstandings: General sadness or disappointment can sometimes be mistaken for the more profound feeling of despair.

CH. 4 EMOTION RELATES:

Emotions found while reading have subtle signs and fictional stories can be likened to embarking on a roller coaster of emotions. These narratives, whether from timeless classics or contemporary literature, are not just about plot and dialogue; they're about the characters' emotional journeys. Applying this understanding to literature and gaining a deeper appreciation for the narrative and even hone own emotional intelligence in your journey...

1. Dialogue:
How characters converse is a direct reflection of their emotional state. Paying attention to what is said, how it's said, and, importantly, what is left unsaid, can offer insights into a character's feelings. For instance, short and curt replies might suggest annoyance, while elaborate, flowing conversations could indicate comfort and intimacy.

2. Descriptive Language:
Authors often employ vivid descriptive language to convey emotions. Phrases like "her eyes sparkled with mischief" or "his shoulders slumped in defeat" paint a clear emotional picture. These subtle cues provide an emotional map, guiding the character's journey.

3. Character's Actions:
Actions, undoubtedly, speak louder than words. A character pacing back and forth might be anxious, while one who frequently checks their watch could be impatient or eager.

4. Inner Thoughts and Monologues:
Many authors give readers a sneak peek into a character's mind. This internal dialogue is a goldmine for understanding emotions. It offers unfiltered access to fears, hopes, regrets, and dreams.

5. Setting and Atmosphere:
The environment in a scene often mirrors the emotional tone. A gloomy, overcast day might set the stage for a sorrowful event, while a bright and sunny backdrop could suggest joy and hope.

6. Interactions with Other Characters:
How a character interacts with others, their reactions, and even their level of engagement can hint at their emotional state. For instance, a character avoiding eye contact might be hiding something or feeling guilty.

7. Symbolism:
Many authors use symbols to represent emotions. A wilting flower might symbolize lost love or fading hope, while a raging storm could represent internal turmoil.

The beauty of fiction is its ability to mirror real emotions and experiences, making it a valuable tool for enhancing emotional understanding. Here are some exercises to help you delve deeper into the emotional fabric of stories and improve your InnerNex application:

1. Character Emotional Journal:
Choose a fictional story or novel you're familiar with.

➲ For a week, pick a character and jot down every emotion they express or experience in different scenes.

➲ At the end of the week, review your journal and identify patterns or triggers for specific emotions.

2. Dialogue Unlocking:
Pick a random page from a book.

➲ Identify dialogues and analyze the emotions conveyed by each character.

➲ Reflect on how the dialogue's tone, pace, and content inform you about the character's feelings.

3. Setting and Atmosphere Analysis:
Read a short story or a chapter from a novel.

➲ List down descriptions of the setting and atmosphere.

➲ Speculate on how these descriptions mirror or contrast the emotions of the characters within that scene.

4. Symbolic Emotion Hunt:
Choose a poem or a short narrative.

➲ Identify symbols used by the author.

➲ Reflect on how these symbols relate to the emotions conveyed in the text.

5. Emotional Role-play:
This works best with a group or partner.

➲ Pick a scene from a play, novel, or short story.

➲ Act out the scene, emphasizing the emotional states of the characters.

➥Discuss with your partner or group the emotions felt and portrayed.

6. Fictional Emotion to Real-life Connection:
Think of a recent event in your life.

➥Find a scene in a novel or story that mirrors the emotions you felt during your personal event.

➥Reflect on the differences and similarities in emotional expression and perception between the fictional character and yourself.

7. Character's Emotional Evolution Chart:
To truly understand the emotional journey of a character from the beginning to the end of a story, it's beneficial to visually map it out. Below is a template you can use to chart out the emotional landscape of your chosen character:

Character Emotional Journey

Title of the Novel:

Character Name:

Chapter/Scene:

Brief Summary:

Primary Emotion:

Secondary Emotion(s):

Triggering Event or Interaction:

Character Response/Action:

Notes/Observations:

End of Novel Reflection:

➥Most Predominant Emotion:

➥Most Significant Emotional Turning Point:

➲ Overall Emotional Evolution of the Character:

➲ Personal Insights Gained:

CH. 5 EMOTIONAL THEMES AND ARCHETYPES IN FICTION:

Every story, regardless of its time or origin, touches upon core human emotions that are universally understood. This universality is often achieved through the use of emotional themes and archetypes. Let's explore some prevalent themes and archetypes and their emotional resonance.

1. The Hero's Journey:
Originated by Joseph Campbell, this theme revolves around a protagonist who undergoes challenges, faces inner and external conflicts, and eventually emerges transformed.
Emotional Spectrum: Courage, fear, determination, doubt, elation, and despair.

2. The Tragic Love:
Stories like Romeo and Juliet or Tristan and Isolde showcase love that faces insurmountable obstacles, often leading to tragedy.
Emotional Spectrum: Passion, longing, sorrow, desperation, hope, and resignation.

3. The Redemption Arc:
Characters, once lost or corrupted, seek redemption and atonement for past mistakes. An example includes Ebenezer Scrooge in "A Christmas Carol."
Emotional Spectrum: Guilt, remorse, hope, enlightenment, gratitude, and relief.

4. The Rite of Passage:
Stories that revolve around milestones or coming-of-age moments, such as "The Catcher in the Rye."
Emotional Spectrum: Curiosity, confusion, defiance, acceptance, growth, and nostalgia.

5. The Quest:
Characters embark on a journey with a specific goal in mind, facing various challenges along the way, as seen in "The Lord of the Rings."
Emotional Spectrum: Determination, wonder, fatigue, camaraderie, temptation, and accomplishment.

6. The Underdog Story:
Stories where the less likely or weaker individual rises against challenges, like "Rocky."

Emotional Spectrum: Hope, inadequacy, perseverance, frustration, triumph, and validation.

7. The Sacrifice:
Characters give up something precious for a greater good or loved one, such as in "The Gift of the Magi."
Emotional Spectrum: Love, conflict, sadness, nobility, regret, and fulfillment.

Understanding emotions in fiction requires a keen sense of observation, an open mind, and the willingness to dive deep into the narrative. Here's a systematic approach to help you navigate and pinpoint emotions in fictional scenarios:

1. Initial Reading:
Start by immersing yourself in the narrative without any preconceived notions. This helps in gaining a holistic view of the story.

2. Note First Impressions:
After your initial read, jot down the emotions you felt during pivotal moments or character interactions. These impressions often align with the author's intention.

3. Character Observation:
Zoom in on the main characters. Ask:

➲ How do they react to certain situations?

➲ What motivates their actions?

➲ Are there patterns in their emotional responses?

4. Dialogue Analysis:
Dialogue often holds emotional undertones. Note the words characters use, their tone, pacing, and any implicit emotions conveyed.

5. Setting and Atmosphere:
Analyze the environment in which events unfold. A gloomy setting might emphasize sadness, while a vibrant one might accentuate happiness or hope.

6. Symbolism and Motifs:
Authors often employ symbols to represent emotions. For instance, a wilting flower might symbolize despair, while a rising sun can indicate hope.

7. Character Relationships:
How characters relate to one another can offer insights into their emotional states. Look for dynamics such as conflict, harmony, dependency, or indifference.

8. Evolution of Emotion:
Track the emotional trajectory of characters. Are they static, or do they evolve? This can

provide depth to their emotional makeup.

9. Cross-reference with Real Life:
Compare fictional emotions with real-life scenarios. Often, authors draw from real experiences, making emotions in fiction relatable.

10. Now, employ the InnerNex method:

➲ Reflect on the primary and secondary emotions.

➲ Analyze the character's response or action following the emotion.

➲ Identify triggers for these emotions.

➲ Draw parallels or contrasts with your own emotional experiences. Learn from reading about impersonal experiences.

11. Reflect and Relate:
How the identified emotions relate to the larger theme of the story. Moreover, consider how these emotions resonate with your own experiences.

12. Discuss with Peers:
Sharing insights and perspectives with fellow readers can provide alternative viewpoints, enriching your understanding of the emotional landscape of the narrative.

By following this systematic approach, you not only enhance your reading experience but also refine your emotional intelligence. Recognizing and understanding emotions in fiction can offer valuable insights into the complex world of human emotions, aiding in real-life scenarios.

CH. 6 EMOTION ANALYSIS IN ACTION BY EXAMPLES:

"The Lonely Lighthouse"

In a small coastal town, there stands an old lighthouse, abandoned for years. Anna, a woman in her mid-30s, finds herself visiting it regularly, staring at the horizon. One day, a storm approaches, but Anna doesn't move. Instead, she climbs to the top, letting the rain drench her as she shouts into the storm.

Emotion Analysis:

> ➥ Primary emotion: Loneliness - Anna's frequent visits to the abandoned lighthouse signify a sense of isolation and seeking solace.

> ➥ Secondary emotion: Desperation - Her act of shouting into the storm showcases an emotional outburst, perhaps a cry for help or an expression of deep-seated pain.

> ➥ Contextual factors: The abandoned lighthouse and the storm symbolize Anna's internal turmoil and desolation.

"The Reunion"

James and Sarah, once childhood best friends, accidentally meet at a coffee shop after two decades. Their conversation is filled with pauses, reflective silences, and subtle smiles. By the end, they promise to meet again, their hands lingering a moment too long as they say goodbye.

Emotion Analysis:

> ➥ Primary emotion: Nostalgia - The reflective silences and subtle smiles indicate a journey down memory lane, reliving the past.

> ➥ Secondary emotion: Hope - The promise to meet again and the prolonged touch suggest a desire to reconnect and perhaps rekindle their bond.

> ➥ Contextual factors: The casual setting of a coffee shop provides a neutral ground, allowing old memories to resurface and new ones to form.

"The Final Verdict"

In a courtroom, a mother listens intently as the verdict for her son's case is about to be announced. Her hands tremble, her breathing is erratic, and her eyes are fixed on the judge. As the word "not guilty" echoes, she collapses into tears.

Emotion Analysis:

➲ Primary emotion: Anxiety - The trembling hands and erratic breathing clearly display the mother's intense nervousness and fear for her son's fate.

➲ Secondary emotion: Relief - The flood of tears following the verdict is a cathartic release from the built-up tension and worry.

➲ Contextual factors: The courtroom setting, with its inherent gravity and the potential life-altering consequences of the verdict, amplifies the emotional stakes.

Recognizing and understanding emotions in narratives is not just an intellectual exercise. By refining these skills, you can transfer them to real-life situations, enhancing interpersonal understanding and communication. Here's how:

1. Active Listening in Conversations:
Just as you would read a fictional piece closely, practice active listening when conversing with others. Pay attention to tone, inflection, and the emotions underlying their words. Delineate non-verbal cues and listen to the speaker's emotional state.

2. Observing Non-Verbal Cues:
Much like noting a character's actions in a story, observing body language, facial expressions, and gestures can give you a clearer picture of a person's emotions, even if they remain unspoken.

3. Asking Open-ended Questions:
Prompt others to share more, as you would dive deeper into a narrative. Open-ended questions can reveal underlying emotions or concerns that may not be immediately evident.

4. Empathetic Responses:
Draw from your understanding of character emotions in fiction and offer responses that show empathy and understanding. Empathetic responses can help build trust and open lines of genuine communication.

5. Self-reflection:
Just as you would analyze a character's motivations and feelings, take time to introspect about your own emotions. Understanding yourself better can improve your interactions with others.

6. Recognizing Emotional Patterns:
If a particular emotion or situation in fiction resonates with you, it might be reflecting a pattern in your own life. Recognizing these patterns can provide insights into your own behaviors and reactions.

7. Enhancing Emotional Vocabulary:
Reading and analyzing emotions in fiction can expand your emotional vocabulary, allowing you to express feelings more accurately and understand others better.

8. Avoiding Assumptions:
Just as you approach a story with an open mind, refrain from making immediate judgments or assumptions about others. Give them space to share, and listen without bias.

9. Using InnerNex in Conflict Resolution:
In disagreements, employ the InnerNex technique to identify primary and secondary emotions in yourself and others. Recognizing these can lead to a more constructive discussion and a quicker resolution.

10. Sharing and Discussing with Others:
Much like discussing fictional scenarios, sharing real-life experiences and feelings with friends or support groups can offer fresh perspectives and deepen emotional understanding.

Harnessing the power of InnerNex in daily interactions can lead to richer, more fulfilling relationships. By translating the skills honed from analyzing fictional emotions to real-world scenarios, you empower yourself to navigate the intricate world of human emotions with clarity and compassion.

Emotion identification, while invaluable, isn't without its complexities in realms of fiction and real life.

1. Ambiguity in Fictional Presentation:
Often, authors leave emotions deliberately vague, allowing readers to interpret based on their own perspectives and life experiences. While this enhances the depth and relatability of a story, it can also present challenges in pinpointing exact emotional states.

Example: A protagonist may stare into the horizon after a significant event. Are they contemplative, melancholic, hopeful, or simply lost in thought?

2. Bias in Real-life Interpretations:
In the real world, personal biases, past experiences, and preconceived notions can cloud judgment. These biases may skew our understanding of another's emotions, leading to misinterpretation or miscommunication.

3. Layers of Emotions:

Both in stories and real life, emotions rarely present themselves in isolation. Jealousy can be underpinned by insecurity; anger might be masking hurt. Unraveling these intertwined emotions requires keen observation and insight.

4. Cultural and Contextual Differences:
A gesture or expression might convey a particular emotion in one culture and an entirely different one in another. Similarly, a fictional setting in a different culture or era can have unique emotional expressions, making interpretation a nuanced process.

5. The Unreliable Narrator in Fiction:
Some stories are told from the perspective of an unreliable narrator, whose portrayal of emotions might be skewed, exaggerated, or even imagined. This adds an extra layer of challenge in emotion identification.

6. Masking Emotions in Reality:
Unlike characters who are bound by the author's portrayal, real individuals might deliberately mask their true feelings, presenting a facade. Detecting the genuine emotion behind the mask requires astute observation and understanding.

7. Subtlety vs. Exaggeration:
While some authors might vividly illustrate a character's emotions, others might use subtlety, requiring readers to "read between the lines." In reality, some people are overt with their emotions, while others are more restrained.

8. Personal Resonance:
Sometimes, a personal emotional experience can resonate so strongly with a fictional scenario or real-life event that it becomes challenging to differentiate between the character's emotions and the reader's own feelings.

9. Emotional Evolution:
As characters grow and narratives progress, their emotional responses might evolve. Similarly, an individual's emotional reactions can change based on life experiences, adding to the challenge of consistent identification.

10. The Complexity of the Human Psyche:
Lastly, the vast range and depth of human emotions, whether in fictional universes or real life, make them intricate to pinpoint accurately consistently. It requires continuous learning, reflection, and open-mindedness.

CH. 7 EMOTION IDENTIFICATION SKILLS:

1. Blind Read:
To identify emotions without relying on explicit emotional descriptors.
Instructions:

➲Read a short passage or excerpt without any explicit emotional words (like 'happy,' 'sad,' 'angry').

➲List down the emotions you believe the characters are experiencing based on context, actions, dialogue, and setting.

➲Compare your interpretation with peers or reference materials to gain different perspectives.

2. Character Journaling:
To deeply understand a character's emotional journey.
Instructions:

➲Choose a character from a novel or short story.

➲After each chapter or significant event, write a journal entry from that character's perspective, focusing on their emotional state.

➲Reflect on how your entries evolve as the story progresses.

3. Emotion Mapping:
To visualize the range and depth of emotions in a narrative.
Instructions:

➲Using a chart, map out the primary and secondary emotions of main characters throughout a story.

➲Reflect on patterns, triggers, and the evolution of these emotions.

4. Role-play:
To embody and express a character's emotions.
Instructions:

➲ Choose a scene from a play, book, or movie.

➲ Act it out, emphasizing the emotional undertones of each character.

➲ Discuss with participants or observers about the emotions portrayed and any differences in interpretations.

5. Rewrite with a Twist:
To understand how changing emotions can alter a narrative.
Instructions:

➲ Select a scene from a book or short story.

➲ Rewrite it by changing the primary emotion of the main character(s).

➲ Reflect on how this change impacts the overall narrative and other characters' reactions.

6. Emotion Flashcards:
To quickly identify and categorize emotions.
Instructions:

➲ Create flashcards with brief fictional scenarios written on them.

➲ On the reverse, write down the intended primary and secondary emotions.

➲ Use these cards for quick drills, trying to identify the emotions before checking the answer.

7. Group Discussions:
To gain multiple perspectives on emotional interpretations.
Instructions:

➲ Read a story or scene in a group.

➲ Discuss each character's emotions, providing evidence from the text to support interpretations.

➲ Note the similarities and differences in each group member's interpretations.

8. Emotional Prediction:
Objective: To anticipate emotional reactions based on narrative cues.

Instructions:

⮑ Pause midway through a novel or movie.

⮑ Predict the upcoming emotional reactions of characters based on the current scenario.

⮑ Resume and compare predictions to the actual narrative.

CH. 8 INTERPRETING EMOTIONAL SIGNALS IN FICTION:

1. Setting and Atmosphere:

    ➲Ambience: A gloomy, rain-soaked street can denote sadness, longing, or mystery. In contrast, a sunlit meadow can evoke feelings of joy, freedom, or nostalgia.

    ➲Time: The narrative's timeframe can also elicit emotions. Dusk might signify endings, melancholy, or reflection, while dawn can represent new beginnings, hope, or rejuvenation.

2. Characters' Physical Expressions:

    ➲Facial Cues: A twitch of an eye, a frown, or a smirk can reveal a lot about what a character feels. Recognizing these nuances helps in empathizing with the character's emotional state.

    ➲Body Language: Slouched shoulders might indicate dejection or exhaustion, while a straight posture can represent confidence or defiance.

3. Dialogue and Monologues:

    ➲What's Said: The choice of words, tone, and pacing can tell a lot. Quick, terse dialogues might denote tension or anger, while long, meandering ones can show reflection or confusion.

    ➲What's Unsaid: Often, the pauses, the unsaid words, or the topics avoided convey deeper emotional undertones than explicit dialogues.

4. Symbolism and Motifs: Literary symbols and recurring motifs can carry emotional weight. For instance, a wilting flower might symbolize lost youth or fleeting beauty.

5. Characters' Actions and Decisions: Often, what characters do, or refrain from doing, mirrors their emotional state. A character might avoid visiting a particular place due to associated traumatic memories.

6. Backstory and Flashbacks: Understanding a character's past provides context to their current emotional state. A tragic past can explain a character's distrust, aloofness, or even their jovial demeanor as a coping mechanism.

7. Narrator's Tone and Perspective: Is the narrator detached or deeply involved? Objective or biased? The narration style can shape the emotional ambiance of the entire narrative.

Emotion-driven Reading Technique: To harness the full power of emotional signals in fiction:

- Don't just read; immerse yourself. Feel the rain, visualize the characters, and put yourself in their shoes.

- Why did a character react a certain way? Is there a hidden motive or emotion?

- After reading, take a moment to reflect on the story's emotional journey. How did it resonate with your experiences or beliefs?

In interpreting these emotional cues, we not only enhance our reading experience but also enrich our emotional vocabulary and understanding.

Ch. 9 **Utilizing InnerNex in Fiction Analysis:**

1. Emotional Identification:

> ➲ Step 1: Skim through a paragraph or scene to get a general sense of the narrative.

> ➲ Step 2: Re-read, this time focusing on key emotional cues – words, phrases, or actions that stand out as emotionally charged.

> ➲ Step 3: List down these cues.

> ➲ Step 4: Reference these cues with the InnerNex to classify the emotions they might signify. For instance, words like "sobbed" or "teary-eyed" can be classified under 'Sadness'.

2. Contextual Understanding:

> ➲ Context is Crucial: The same word might convey different emotions in different contexts. For example, 'bright' could indicate happiness in one scenario and surprise in another.

> ➲ Backtracking: If an emotion feels unclear, trace back to previous chapters or scenes for a better context.

3. Character Emotional Arc Mapping:

> ➲ Step 1: Choose a primary character.

> ➲ Step 2: Map out their emotional journey using the InnerNex, noting highs and lows and the events leading to these emotional states.

> ➲ Step 3: This mapping can provide insights into character development and depth.

4. Thematic Analysis:

> ➲ Step 1: Identify the central themes of the story.

> ➲ Step 2: Utilize the InnerNex to determine how emotions play into these themes, highlighting the emotional undercurrents that drive the narrative.

5. Comparative Emotional Analysis:

> ➲ Step 1: Select two (or more) characters or scenes.

> ➲ Step 2: Compare and contrast their emotional signals using the InnerNex method. This can provide a more profound understanding of relational dynamics or

narrative contrasts.

6. Personal Reflection and Connection:

➲ After analyzing the text, take a moment to reflect on how the identified emotions resonate with your feelings or experiences. The InnerNex can serve as a mirror, reflecting our emotional responses to fictional scenarios.

InnerNex-Driven Group Discussions: Group discussions can further enrich the analysis:

➲ Share your InnerNex findings with peers.

➲ Engage in debates over ambiguous emotional signals.

➲ Collaborate to map out intricate emotional webs in complex narratives.

CH. 10 EMOTION EXERCISES AND PRACTICE SCENARIOS:

Exercise 1: Quick Recognition and speed up your emotion identification prowess.

Step 1: Read the following short sentences and quickly determine the primary emotion being depicted.

➲ "She squealed and clapped, her eyes wide with joy."

➲ "His heart raced as he hid behind the curtains."

➲ "A single tear rolled down as she looked at the old photograph."

Exercise 2: Deep Dive into Context and understand how context can alter the emotion perceived.

Scenario: "Sarah looked at the letter, her hands shaking."

Question: Why are Sarah's hands shaking? Provide three different emotions based on varying contexts.

Possible Answers:

➲ Anticipation: Sarah has been waiting for this acceptance letter from her dream university.

➲ Fear: Sarah recognized the handwriting, and it was from someone she wished never to hear from again.

➲ Joy: The letter was from her long-lost brother, reaching out after years.

Exercise 3: Character Emotion Arc and trace the emotional journey of a character.

Scenario: Choose a short story or a chapter from a novel. Select a primary character and chart their emotional states using the InnerNex as they navigate through the narrative.

Exercise 4: Emotion Density in Scenes and determine which scenes are emotionally charged and why.

Scenario: Read a chapter from any novel. Identify the scenes with the highest emotional density using the InnerNex method. Discuss the narrative significance of these emotionally intense scenes.

Exercise 5: Personal Reflection and connect the emotions in the narrative to personal experiences.

Scenario: Think of a recent book you've read. Using the InnerNex method, pinpoint a scene that resonated deeply with you. Reflect on why this scene was impactful and if it mirrors any of your personal experiences or emotions.
Answer to Exercise 1 Step 1:

- Joy

- Fear

- Sadness

Over time, with regular practice, discerning the intricate emotional undertones in narratives will become second nature. This art of emotional understanding.

CH. 11 ADVANCED INNERNEX TECHNIQUES AND TIPS:

1. Subtext and Reading Between the Lines:

    ➲Often, emotions aren't stated explicitly. They lurk in the shadows, between the lines, waiting to be discovered.

    ➲Always be alert to what's *not* being said. Silence, pauses, and omitted information can be as revealing as explicit statements.

2. The Ripple Effect:

    ➲Emotions can ripple through a narrative. One event can set off a chain reaction of emotions that affect multiple characters or even the setting itself.

    ➲After a significant event, trace how various characters react emotionally. Observe how these reactions evolve as the story progresses.

3. Contrasts and Juxtapositions:

    ➲Authors often place contrasting emotions side by side to amplify the impact or to highlight a particular theme or character trait.

    ➲Be on the lookout for scenes where happiness is juxtaposed with sadness, fear with courage, or love with hate. This technique can provide profound insights into the heart of the narrative.

4. Recurring Emotional Motifs:

    ➲Motifs are recurring elements in a story. When these motifs are tied to emotions, they can offer consistent emotional touchpoints throughout the narrative.

    ➲Identify and track recurring motifs. Understand the emotional significance they carry and how they evolve over the narrative.

5. The Setting as an Emotional Barometer:

    ➲Sometimes, the environment or setting of a story mirrors the emotions of the characters. A stormy night might coincide with a character's internal turmoil, for instance.

➲ Always consider the setting's emotional tone. Is the environment complementing or contrasting the characters' feelings?

6. Beyond Words: The Role of Punctuation and Structure:

➲ The way sentences are constructed, and the punctuation used can hint at underlying emotions.

➲ A series of short, abrupt sentences might indicate tension or panic. On the other hand, long, meandering sentences could suggest contemplation or confusion.

These advanced techniques will elevate your comprehension and appreciation of emotions in fiction. It's akin to equipping yourself with a magnifying glass, allowing you to observe the subtlest of emotional nuances.

CH. 12 INNERNEX IN MODERN MEDIA:

The emotional arcs in movies, TV shows, and other digital narratives are just as intricate, if not more so, given the added layers of visual and auditory cues.Modern media demands a slightly different lens, one that integrates visual, auditory, and narrative cues.

1. Visual Cues and Emotional Resonance:

    ◓Unlike textual narratives, movies and TV shows offer visual cues — facial expressions, body language, color palettes, and even lighting can hint at a character's emotional state.

    ◓While watching a scene, pay attention to a character's facial expressions. The subtlest of eyebrow raises, smirks, or teary eyes can reveal a wealth of emotion. Similarly, body language — a clenched fist, a hunched posture, or an exuberant jump — speaks volumes.

2. Auditory Signals:

    ◓The background score, dialogues' tone, and even silence can serve as significant emotional indicators in modern media.

    ◓Listen for the background music's tempo and instrument choice. A melancholic violin might indicate sadness, while upbeat drums might suggest excitement. Silence, especially when prolonged, can emphasize tension, uncertainty, or contemplation.

3. Cinematography and Emotion:

    ◓The way scenes are shot can influence how emotions are perceived. Close-ups can provide an intimate look into a character's feelings, while long shots might indicate isolation or detachment.

    ◓Observe the camera angles and movements. A shaky camera might suggest chaos or panic, while a steady, slow pan might be used to build suspense or showcase a character's contemplation.

4. The Role of Setting and Environment:

⮱Just as in textual narratives, the setting in visual media plays a crucial role in mirroring or contrasting emotions.

⮱Pay attention to the locations chosen. A bustling city might indicate the chaos and pace of life, while a serene lakeside might hint at peace, reflection, or solitude.

5. Dialogues and Subtext:

⮱What characters say, how they say it, and what they choose not to say can all provide insights into their emotional world.

⮱Listen closely to dialogues, especially in emotionally charged scenes. The choice of words, the pauses, the tone — they all weave together to form the emotional fabric of the scene.

6. Genre and Emotional Themes:

⮱Different genres tend to explore specific emotional themes. Horror delves into fear, while romances explore love, longing, and sometimes heartbreak.

⮱Understanding the genre can set initial emotional expectations, allowing for a more refined InnerNex analysis as you recognize deviations or unique genre-blending moments.

CH. 13 REAL-LIFE APPLICATION:

1. The Link Between Reading and Empathy:

➥Numerous studies have shown that individuals who read fiction regularly are better at understanding others' emotions, thoughts, and feelings. This is because fiction provides a safe space for readers to step into another person's shoes.

➥When reading, immerse yourself fully. Feel the protagonist's joy, sorrow, or anger. This trains the empathetic muscles in the brain, making them more responsive in real-life situations.

2. InnerNex as a Training Tool:

➥Just as one would use a workout regimen to train their body, InnerNex can serve as a regimen for the mind. By continually applying it while reading or watching media, one is essentially practicing the art of emotional recognition.

➥Dedicate specific reading sessions where the sole focus is on applying InnerNex. Over time, this targeted practice will enhance one's natural ability to pick up on emotional cues in real life.

3. Improving Social Interactions:

➥Recognizing and understanding emotions is crucial for effective communication. By applying InnerNex's principles in real-life conversations, one can navigate complex social scenarios with ease.

➥During conversations, be observant. Notice the other person's tone, body language, and choice of words. This will provide deeper insights into their emotional state, allowing for more empathetic responses.

4. Conflict Resolution:

➥Emotions often run high during conflicts. Understanding these emotions is the key to resolving disagreements in a constructive manner.

➥When faced with conflict, take a moment to apply InnerNex. Understand the underlying emotions — be it frustration, sadness, or disappointment. Addressing these emotions directly often paves the way for productive conversations.

5. Strengthening Personal Relationships:

➲ Personal relationships, be it with family, friends, or partners, thrive on understanding and emotional support. InnerNex can be a valuable tool in deepening these bonds.

➲ Take time to understand the emotional needs and states of loved ones. Regularly check in with them, not just through words but by observing their emotional cues. This deepens trust and fosters stronger connections.

The beauty of InnerNex lies in its versatility. A tool to decode fictional emotions, applying its potential applications in real-life scenarios are vast and invaluable. One can cultivate deeper connections, resolve conflicts amicably, and grow overall social and emotional intelligence.

CH. 14 YOUR INNER JOURNEY:

1. InnerNex Reading Sessions:

➲ Dedicate specific reading times to focus solely on identifying and understanding emotions. Choose diverse reading materials to challenge and refine your emotional discernment.

➲ Begin with short stories or passages. As you read, jot down emotions you identify. Once done, compare your list with a partner or a discussion group.

2. Movie Analysis Nights:

➲ Movies, with their visual and auditory elements, offer a comprehensive platform to practice InnerNex.

➲ Watch a movie or a show episode. Pause during intense emotional scenes and discuss or jot down the emotions on display. Analyze the reasons behind the characters' feelings, using context clues.

3. Daily Emotion Journaling:

➲ A personal reflection exercise to identify and understand your own emotions throughout the day.

➲ At the end of each day, note down significant emotional experiences. Delve into the reasons behind each emotion and how they impacted your behavior.

4. InnerNex Role-Playing:

➲ Engage in role-playing sessions where participants emulate different characters and scenarios, emphasizing emotional display and recognition.

➲ Create scenarios, assign roles, and let participants interact. Afterward, discuss the emotional dynamics at play.

5. Empathetic Listening Practice:

➲ Enhance real-life InnerNex application by actively listening to someone and identifying their emotions.

◗Engage in deep conversations with friends or family. Focus on their tone, body language, and content. After the conversation, reflect on the emotions you recognized.

6. InnerNex in Art:

◗Art, whether paintings, sculptures, or music, carries deep emotional content. Analyzing art can be a fun way to practice InnerNex.

◗Visit a museum or an art gallery. Dedicate time to individual pieces and identify the emotions they evoke. Discuss interpretations with fellow attendees.

7. Flash Fiction InnerNex:

◗ Challenge yourself with ultra-short stories and gauge the emotions in just a few lines.

◗Find or write flash fiction pieces. Read them and quickly jot down the emotions you identify. This exercise helps in sharpening swift emotional discernment.

CH. 15 INNERNEX APPLICATION:

1. Recognizing Emotions in Conversations:

Just as in fiction, real-world dialogues are filled with hidden emotions. Utilizing InnerNex, we can pick up subtle cues, inflections, and the unsaid words that may reveal more about a person's emotional state.

Practical Tips:

- Listen more than you speak.

- Note the choice of words and tonality.

- Understand the context.

2. Emotion in Written Communications:

From emails to messages, our digital age communication tools lack the tonality of spoken words. Here's how InnerNex can be a crucial tool.

Practical Tips:

- Look for emotionally charged words.

- Understand the context and background of the conversation.

- Avoid jumping to conclusions; instead, ask open-ended questions to grasp the true emotion.

3. Real-time Responses using InnerNex:

Once we recognize emotions, the next step is to respond. Responding with emotional intelligence ensures healthy relationships and mutual understanding.

Practical Tips:

➲ Take a moment before responding.

➲ Use "I feel" statements.

Validate the other person's emotions without necessarily agreeing.

4. InnerNex in Professional Environments:

The workplace can be a melting pot of emotions. How can InnerNex
help in navigating professional relationships?

Practical Tips:

➲ Understand that every individual may have different emotional triggers.

➲ Foster an environment of open communication.

➲ Use InnerNex in team meetings to ensure emotional well-being.

5. Continuous Learning and Application:

As with any skill, the application of InnerNex requires practice. Continuous
application in different scenarios will enhance proficiency.

Practical Tips:

➲ Regularly reflect on interactions.

➲ Seek feedback.

➲ Engage in InnerNex exercises to sharpen skills.

We can improve our interpersonal relationships, enhance communication, and cultivate
a deeper understanding of those around us. Knowing the colorful world of emotions.

CH. 16 LIFE IN ACTION:

At The Workplace

Anna, a project manager, noticed tensions rising among her team members. Using her InnerNex skills, she identified signs of frustration, stress, and miscommunication.

By recognizing these emotions, Anna organized a team meeting. During this, she addressed the unspoken emotions and encouraged open communication. As a result, a major project bottleneck was identified and resolved.

Improved team dynamics, better communication, and a successfully completed project on time.

In Relationships

Mark and Lisa, married for five years, often found themselves in arguments. Lisa, familiar with InnerNex, noticed patterns of unrecognized emotions in their disagreements.

Lisa realized that their arguments often stemmed from unaddressed insecurities. Instead of reacting defensively, she started addressing the underlying emotions, leading to more profound and constructive discussions.

Enhanced understanding between the couple, leading to a healthier and more harmonious relationship.

Educational Setting

Mr. Roberts, a high school teacher, was concerned about a student, Danny, who seemed disengaged and isolated.

Mr. Roberts, using his InnerNex skills, identified signs of anxiety and fear in Danny's behavior. Instead of reprimanding him, Mr. Roberts provided a safe space for Danny to express his concerns.

Danny confided about being bullied, leading to timely intervention and support, ensuring a safer learning environment.

In Social Interactions

During a friend's dinner party, Sarah noticed Jane, a fellow guest, constantly checking her phone and appearing distant.

Instead of judging Jane as rude or uninterested, Sarah identified signs of worry and concern. Approaching Jane empathetically, Sarah learned that Jane was dealing with a family emergency.

Sarah's understanding gesture provided Jane with much-needed support, fostering a deep bond between the two.

Recognizing and understanding emotions allows for empathetic interactions, effective problem-solving, and fostering genuine connections.

CH. 17 ADVANCED TECHNIQUES AND CHALLENGES IN INNERNEX APPLICATION:

1. The Layering Technique

Emotions in texts can often be layered, meaning there's more than one emotion at play.

Look for clusters of emotional indicators. For instance, if a character says, "I am thrilled about my promotion, but I can't shake off the feeling of sadness," there's a combination of happiness and sadness.

These can sometimes be contradictory, making them hard to pinpoint.

2. Contextual Analysis

The context can alter the emotional meaning of words.

Always consider the broader situation. For example, "He's cold" in a story about winter has a different emotional connotation than in a narrative about a distant boyfriend.

It's easy to take phrases at face value, potentially leading to misinterpretations.

3. Subtextual Reading

Often, the most profound emotions are those that remain unsaid.

Look for what's *not* being said. If a character talks extensively about everything but their failing marriage, that's a significant emotional indicator.

It requires an intuitive reading style, which can be subjective.

4. Emotional Evolution

Characters, like real people, evolve emotionally.

Track emotional arcs. If a character starts a story feeling defeated but shows signs of hope by the end, that's a transformative journey.

Keeping track of subtle emotional shifts across a narrative can be daunting.

5. Navigating Ambiguity

Some texts purposefully maintain emotional ambiguity to provoke thought.

Instead of pinning down a singular emotion, consider the range of possibilities. A character's statement, "I don't know how I feel about this," can open a spectrum of emotions from confusion to apprehension.

Embracing ambiguity can feel unsatisfying, especially when one is seeking definitive answers.

6. Emotional Intensity and Nuance

Not all emotions are felt with the same intensity.

Look for intensity markers. Words like "slightly," "overwhelmed," or "a tad" can modulate the depth of the emotion being expressed.

Overlooking these markers can lead to overestimation or underestimation of emotional intensity.

CH. 18 INNERNEX IN DIFFERENT LITERARY GENRES:

Understanding the genre's emotional spectrum aids in the more nuanced and effective use of your InnerNex. Every literary genre offers a unique palette of emotions.

1. Romance

Strong emotions revolving around love, passion, betrayal, and longing.

Look for emotional intensifiers. Words like "burning," "aching," or "yearning" frequently indicate heightened emotional states.

2. Mystery/Thriller

Suspense, curiosity, fear, and surprise dominate.

Pay attention to pacing. Rapid sequences of events might amplify feelings of anxiety or anticipation. A character's internal monologue can provide valuable emotional insight into their psychological state.

3. Fantasy

A mix of wonder, bravery, fear, and the confrontation of good vs. evil.

Given the often otherworldly contexts, emotions might manifest differently. For instance, an elf's sense of sadness might be expressed differently than a human's. InnerNex can help bridge the gap between the unfamiliar and the relatable.

4. Science Fiction

Exploration of the unknown, moral dilemmas, and the emotional ramifications of technological advancements.

Emotions may be intertwined with speculative elements. A character's reaction to a futuristic scenario can offer a deep dive into complex feelings about humanity, ethics, and progress.

5. Historical Fiction

Rooted in real events, this genre offers a blend of nostalgia, reverence, and sometimes, cultural clashes.

Emotions can be tied to historical contexts. A character's joy in one era might be sourced from events or milestones unrelatable to contemporary readers. Using InnerNex, one can unearth these contextually rooted emotions.

6. Horror

Dominated by fear, dread, shock, and sometimes, morbid curiosity.

Focus on sensory descriptions. The sound of a creaking floorboard or the sight of a shadow can invoke profound fear. InnerNex can gauge the depth and nature of this fear, separating genuine terror from mere unease.

7. Drama

Often revolves around interpersonal relationships, internal conflicts, and societal issues.

Emotions are central to drama. By scrutinizing dialogues and internal reflections using InnerNex, one can gauge the undercurrents of emotions driving the narrative.

CH. 19 EMOTIONS BEYOND WORDS:

1. Body Language

A character's physical stance and movements can unveil their true feelings. For instance:

- Crossed Arms: Might indicate defensiveness or discomfort.

- Fidgeting: Nervousness or impatience.

- A long stare: Deep contemplation or challenge.

By tuning into these non-verbal cues, readers can glean a deeper understanding of a character's emotional landscape.

2. Environment and Atmosphere

The setting can be a powerful tool to evoke and represent emotions. A gloomy, rainy day can symbolize sadness or introspection, while a bright, sunny day might indicate happiness or a new beginning. Observing the environment can offer a contextual layer to the characters' emotions.

3. Interactions with Objects

Sometimes, a character's relationship with an inanimate object can reveal a lot about their internal state. For example, a character tightly gripping a locket might be reminiscing or mourning a loss.

4. Pauses and Silence

The absence of dialogue or action can be telling. Silence can signify tension, contemplation, or a pivotal emotional moment. Recognizing the weight of these pauses can provide deeper emotional clarity.

5. Flashbacks and Memories

When a character is lost in thought or revisits a past event, it often holds emotional significance. These memories can be joyful, traumatic, or bittersweet, offering a window into the character's past experiences and emotional baggage.

6. Symbolism

Authors often use symbols to represent emotions. A wilting flower might signify lost youth or fading love, while a soaring bird could symbolize freedom or aspiration. Identifying and interpreting these symbols enhances the InnerNex experience.

Tuning into these silent cues requires a heightened level of awareness and empathy. However, mastering this skill can transform a reading experience, making it richer and more immersive.

CH. 20 CONNECTING WITH CHARACTERS: THE INNERNEX WAY:

1. Empathetic Reading

Understanding a character's emotions is more than just recognizing what they're feeling; it's about deeply resonating with their experiences.

> *Tip*: Visualize yourself in the character's shoes. How would you react? What would you feel in that exact moment?

2. Reflect and Relate

Often, characters' experiences can mirror our own, albeit in a fictional setting. Recognizing these parallels can deepen the connection.

> *Tip*: After a significant event in the story, pause and reflect on a time when you felt similarly. It helps in internalizing the character's emotions.

3. Dialogue

Conversations in fiction aren't just exchanges of information. They're rife with emotions, hidden meanings, and subtext.

> *Tip*: When analyzing dialogues, look beyond the words. What isn't being said? Is there any underlying tension or unsaid affection?

4. Emotional Journaling

Maintaining a journal can be an effective way to track and reflect on the myriad emotions encountered while reading.

> *Tip*: After each reading session, jot down the primary emotions you felt or identified. Over time, you'll notice patterns, helping in refining your InnerNex

skills.

5. Analyzing Character Arcs

Characters evolve, and so do their emotions. Tracking their journey and emotional growth offers deeper insights.

- *Tip*: At significant plot milestones, assess the character's emotional state. How have they changed since the beginning? What events triggered these changes?

6. Engage with Fellow Readers

Discussing a book with others offers varied emotional perspectives, enriching your understanding.

> ❐*Tip*: Join book clubs or online forums. Different readers will resonate with different aspects of the story, broadening your emotional horizon.

By intertwining InnerNex practices with the process of reading, you not only enhance your fictional journey but also fortify your real-world emotional intelligence. Feeling stories on a whole new level.

CH. 21 CHALLENGES AND SOLUTIONS:

Fear not! For every challenge, there is a solution waiting to be discovered!!

1. Challenge: Overwhelm

It's easy to feel overwhelmed, especially when faced with a complex narrative rich in emotional depth.

Solution: Start small. Instead of diving into a full-length novel, begin with short stories or even children's books. These typically present emotions in a more straightforward manner, allowing you to build your confidence.

2. Challenge: Misidentification

Sometimes, what seems like one emotion might be another in disguise. For instance, pride can sometimes mask insecurity.

Solution: Always consider context. Dive deeper into the background, environment, and past experiences of the character. This will give you a broader perspective and help in accurate identification.

3. Challenge: Emotional Bias

Your own emotions and experiences can color your perception, causing you to interpret a character's feelings based on your own biases.

Solution: Practice objectivity. Step back and analyze the text from a neutral standpoint. Asking others for their interpretation can also provide new insights.

4. Challenge: Language Barriers

When exploring literature from different cultures, emotions might be presented in ways unfamiliar to you.

Solution: Educate yourself about cultural nuances and emotional expressions in different societies. This broadens your understanding and ensures you don't misinterpret emotions based on cultural differences.

5. Challenge: Complexity of Human Emotion

Emotions aren't always clear-cut. Characters, like real people, can experience multiple emotions simultaneously.

Solution: Embrace the complexity. Instead of trying to fit an emotion into a single category, allow for the possibility of layered emotions. Your InnerNex chart can always be expanded to include combinations.

6. Challenge: Overthinking

There's a tendency to overanalyze, which can cloud intuitive understanding.

Solution: Trust your instincts. Sometimes, the first emotional response you discern from a text is the right one. Over time, your intuition will become one of your strongest tools.

Remember, every challenge is an opportunity in disguise. The hurdles you face while honing your InnerNex skills will only refine your understanding and deepen your connection to the narratives you explore.

CH. 22 APPLIED INNERNEX: REAL-WORLD SCENARIOS:

1. Personal Relationships:

Scenario: Your friend has been unusually quiet during a group gathering.

InnerNex Application: Recall instances from literature where a character displays reticence. Consider the emotions behind such behaviors. Could it be anxiety, preoccupation, or perhaps an underlying sadness? Approach your friend with empathy, and you might open a channel of communication that allows them to express their feelings.

2. Professional Settings:

Scenario: A coworker sharply disagrees with a point you've made during a meeting.

Think about conflicts in literature and the emotions driving them. Is your coworker's disagreement stemming from professional concern, personal insecurities, or a combination of both? This analysis helps you address the actual issue without escalating tensions.

3. Social Media Interactions:

Someone posts a strongly worded opinion on a topic you care about.

Online environments, much like fictional ones, have a layer of detachment. By analyzing the emotion behind the words (anger, passion, desperation), you can craft a more measured and constructive response.

4. Everyday Encounters:

A stranger in a store appears distressed.

Drawing parallels with fictional scenarios, you might deduce they're feeling overwhelmed, anxious, or lost. Offering assistance or a kind word could make all the difference in their day.

5. Global Events:

You're watching news coverage of a significant event.

News narratives are richly imbued with emotions. By analyzing these emotions, you can better understand the event's impact on people and communities. This insight fosters empathy and informed discussions.

CH. 23 EXAMPLES & EXERCISES:

Scenario 1: Lucy stood at the edge of the pier, staring into the distance. The waves gently lapped at the shores, and the setting sun painted the sky in hues of orange and pink. A folded letter lay beside her, its edges fluttering in the wind.

The scene is serene with the setting sun and gentle waves, but Lucy's action of standing at the edge and the presence of the folded letter suggest contemplation, nostalgia, or perhaps sadness.

Based on the given scenario, list down three emotions Lucy might be feeling and provide reasons for each.

Scenario 2: At the crowded marketplace, Mark bumped into a man, causing him to drop a bag of apples. Instead of helping, Mark hurriedly walked away, avoiding eye contact.

The avoidance of eye contact and the hurried pace indicate feelings of guilt or embarrassment on Mark's part.

Write a short paragraph from Mark's perspective detailing his thoughts and emotions after the incident.

Scenario 3: Elena opened her birthday gift from her best friend, expecting the book she had hinted at for months. Instead, she found a hand-knit scarf. She smiled, her eyes glistening with tears.

Elena's reaction to the scarf indicates surprise followed by deep appreciation and emotion, showing that it's the thought and effort that count more than the gift itself.

Describe a situation in your life where an unexpected gesture evoked a strong emotional response.

After days of trekking through the dense forest, Amelia finally reached the clearing. Overcome with relief and fatigue, she dropped to her knees and looked up, thanking the stars.

Amelia's journey indicates persistence and determination. Reaching the clearing brings emotions of relief, gratitude, and exhaustion.

Recall a moment of achievement in your life. Write a short narrative detailing the emotions leading up to and following that moment.

These scenarios serve as practice fields. Practicing them, you hone your InnerNex proficiency, sharpening your ability to decode and understand the emotions at play in various situations.

CH. 24 APPLICATIONS BEYOND FICTION:

1. Personal Relationships:
InnerNex can assist in understanding the emotions of loved ones better. By honing the skills to detect subtle emotional cues, one can be more empathetic, responsive, and supportive.

Example: Consider a friend who's narrating a recent experience. By applying InnerNex techniques, you could potentially discern underlying emotions even if they aren't openly expressed, leading to deeper, more empathetic conversations.

2. Professional Settings:
In the workplace, understanding the emotions of colleagues can foster better collaboration. InnerNex can help managers and team members alike to navigate and respond to emotional cues, promoting a harmonious work environment.

Example: During team meetings, analyzing the sentiments behind the words of colleagues can lead to a more effective response, be it in conflict resolution or in motivating team members.

3. Education:
Teachers can utilize InnerNex to better understand students' emotions, tailoring their teaching methods accordingly. Recognizing a student's frustration or enthusiasm can significantly impact their educational journey.

If a teacher identifies that a student feels anxious every time they're asked to read aloud, they can provide additional support or alternative methods to make the student more comfortable.

4. Consumer Behavior:
Marketers and business owners can benefit from InnerNex by assessing the emotional responses of consumers to products, advertisements, or brand messages. This can guide effective strategy planning.

In focus group discussions, InnerNex can be used to ascertain the genuine emotional response of participants towards a new product advertisement.

5. Self-awareness and Personal Growth:
Lastly, and perhaps most crucially, InnerNex can be a tool for introspection. Regularly practicing InnerNex on fictional scenarios can train the mind to be more attuned to one's emotions, fostering self-awareness.

Reflecting on personal experiences and journaling emotions, as suggested earlier, can lead to a clearer understanding of one's emotional patterns and triggers.

Scenario 1: The Draft Letter

Tom was engrossed in the latest Beatles record when a sharp knock interrupted. He opened the door to find a stern-looking postman. Handing over an official-looking envelope, he said, "You might want to read this right away." Tom's hands shook as he read. The draft board had called his number.

InnerNex Analysis:

> ●Setting: The Beatles, indicative of the '60s and the cultural revolution of that era.

> ●Action: An unexpected letter from the draft board, indicative of the Vietnam War draft.

> ●Physical Reaction: Tom's hands shaking indicates fear or anxiety.

> ●Possible Emotions: Dread, surprise, apprehension.

Scenario 2: Breaking the Glass Ceiling

Angela adjusted her shoulder pads and took a deep breath. It was the '80s, and she was about to walk into a board meeting, the first woman to do so at her company. As she stepped in, several men looked up, their expressions ranging from curious to skeptical.

InnerNex Analysis:

> ●Setting: The '80s, a period of increasing corporate and gender dynamics.

> ●Action: Angela entering a male-dominated space, symbolic of breaking barriers.

> ●Physical Reaction: Taking a deep breath indicates preparation and determination.

> ●Possible Emotions: Courage, determination, a touch of anxiety.

Scenario 3: The Fall of the Wall

As news of the Berlin Wall's fall spread in 1989, Maria, having migrated from East Germany a decade earlier, sat in her American apartment, eyes glued to the TV. Tears streamed down her face as she watched familiar streets now free, memories flooding back.

InnerNex Analysis:

- Setting: The historical event of the Berlin Wall's fall.

- Action: Maria's reminiscence of her homeland and the significance of the event.

- Physical Reaction: Tears, an overwhelming emotional response.

- Possible Emotions: Joy, nostalgia, relief, sorrow for the lost years.

Scenario 4: Millennial Memories

In the early 2000s, Jake logged into his MSN Messenger, eagerly awaiting a ping. As the familiar notification sounded, he saw a message from his school crush. Heart racing, he responded with a custom emoticon, hoping to impress.

InnerNex Analysis:

- Setting: Early 2000s, the rise of instant messaging and digital communication.

- Action: Jake's interaction with his crush via MSN, a typical teenage experience of that era.

- Physical Reaction: Heart racing in excitement or nervousness.

- Possible Emotions: Anticipation, excitement, nervousness.

CH. 25 USING INNERNEX TO PREDICT CHARACTER ACTIONS:

Understanding a fictional character's emotions often leads us to predict their subsequent actions. By observing the emotional cues, a pattern emerges, linking emotions to behaviors. Let's delve into some textual scenarios to practice this predictive approach:

Scenario 1: The Heartbreak

Ellen stood by the window, gazing out at the pouring rain. The letter, now crumpled in her hand, contained words she never thought she'd read: "It's over." She remembered their promises, the late-night talks, and the vacations planned. A tear slipped down her cheek.

InnerNex Analysis:

- Setting: Rainy ambiance, often associated with gloom or sadness.

- Action: The receipt of a breakup letter.

- Physical Reaction: Tear rolling down.

- Emotions: Sadness, disbelief, perhaps a hint of anger or betrayal.

- Predicted Action: Ellen might reminisce more, confront the person who wrote the letter, or seek comfort from a friend.

Scenario 2: The Big Opportunity

Lee's eyes widened as he scanned the email. The national writing competition he'd entered had selected his piece as a finalist! He felt a rush of elation, the hours of hard work finally paying off. On his desk lay three other unfinished stories.

InnerNex Analysis:

- Setting: A quiet workspace.

- Action: The receipt of an acceptance email.

- Physical Reaction: Eyes widening in surprise.

◯ Emotions: Elation, pride, satisfaction.

◯ Predicted Action: Lee might start working on finishing the other stories, share the news with friends and family, or take a moment to celebrate.

Scenario 3: The Unexpected Reunion

As Carla walked through the busy marketplace, a familiar voice called her name. Turning around, she saw Rosa, her childhood best friend, whom she hadn't seen in two decades. Their last parting hadn't been amicable.

InnerNex Analysis:

◯ Setting: A bustling marketplace.

◯ Action: An unexpected reunion.

◯ Physical Reaction: Surprised recognition.

◯ Emotions: Surprise, nostalgia, hesitancy due to their past.

◯ Predicted Action: Carla might approach Rosa and start a conversation, addressing their past, or she might choose to avoid her due to their history.

Through these scenarios, we're not only understanding emotions but using them as a foundation to predict possible future actions of characters. This deepens our engagement with the story, making reading an interactive experience.

CH. 26 DECIPHERING COMPLEX EMOTIONS WITH INNERNEX:

Scenario 1: The Unexpected Gift

Andrea's birthday was a low-key affair this year. She wasn't expecting any surprises. But when her colleague, whom she had a disagreement with just last week, handed her a beautifully wrapped gift, her feelings were mixed.

InnerNex Analysis:

> ➲ Setting: A birthday celebration.

> ➲ Action: Receiving an unexpected gift.

> ➲ Emotions: Surprise due to the unexpected gesture, gratitude for the gift, confusion stemming from their recent disagreement, and skepticism about the colleague's intentions.

Scenario 2: The Bittersweet Win

Danny had practiced for years, and tonight he stood as the champion of the national chess tournament. Yet, the empty chair where his late father used to sit, his biggest supporter, cast a shadow on his victory.

InnerNex Analysis:

> ➲ Setting: Victory in a chess tournament.

> ➲ Action: Triumph contrasted with the absence of a loved one.

> ➲ Emotions: Pride in his achievement, sadness from the loss of his father, longing wishing his father could see his success, and a touch of loneliness.

Scenario 3: The Long-Awaited Promotion

Claire was offered the promotion she'd been vying for, but it came with a twist: a relocation to another country. While the job was a dream come true, moving would mean leaving her aging parents behind.

InnerNex Analysis:

➲ Setting: A workplace announcement.

➲ Action: A promotion coupled with relocation.

➲ Emotions: Elation at the job opportunity, apprehension about the move, concern for her parents, and a sense of dilemma over her choice.

CH. 27 INNERNEX IN PLAY:

This exercise section aims to cultivate an intuitive understanding of emotions, deepening the skill in InnerNex analysis.

Exercise 1: The Surprise Reunion

Sarah walked into the café, hoping to grab a quick coffee. As she scanned for a seat, her eyes landed on a familiar face from her past – James, her high school sweetheart, whom she hadn't seen in over 10 years. He noticed her and waved with a smile.

Your InnerNex Analysis:

        Setting:
        Action:
        Emotions:

Answer:

➲ Setting: A casual café.

➲ Action: A surprise reunion with a high school sweetheart.

➲ Emotions: Surprise, nostalgia, curiosity, a hint of excitement.

Exercise 2: The Lost and Found

Mia had always cherished the locket her grandmother gave her. One day, after coming back from a hike, she realized it was missing. Distraught, she retraced her steps, and just when she was about to give up, a young boy approached her, holding out the precious locket.

Your InnerNex Analysis:

        Setting:
        Action:
        Emotions:

Answer:

➲ Setting: Outdoors after a hike.

➲ Action: Losing a cherished item and then unexpectedly finding it.

➲ Emotions: Panic, despair, relief, gratitude.

Exercise 3: The Unread Messages

Brian woke up to find his phone flooded with messages. As he skimmed through, he found out he had won a photography contest he'd entered on a whim. Before he could let the news sink in, another message popped up: his sister had given birth to twins.

Your InnerNex Analysis:

> Setting:
> Action:
> Emotions:

Answer:

➲ Setting: Morning time in Brian's home.

➲ Action: Discovering unexpected news on the phone.

➲ Emotions: Overwhelm, elation, surprise, joy.

Remember that emotions are multidimensional. While the answers provided give a structured response, individual interpretations based on personal experiences and perspectives can vary.

CH. 28 FINE-TUNING YOUR INNERNEX SKILLS:

Having worked through various exercises, the next step is refining your skills to make your InnerNex analysis more nuanced and accurate. Let's explore some advanced techniques to elevate your understanding and application.

1. Context is King

Understanding the broader context of a fictional scenario can give richer meaning to the emotions that are being conveyed. For example:

"As Mark stood at the edge of the cliff, he spread his arms and took in the vast horizon."

Here, if we know that Mark has recently overcome a significant personal challenge, the emotions felt might be triumph, relief, or liberation.

2. Subtle Differences

Understanding the fine line between similar emotions can make a big difference. Consider the nuances between:

- Contentment vs. Happiness
- Jealousy vs. Envy
- Pride vs. Arrogance

3. The Role of Cultural Influences

Cultural backgrounds can deeply influence how emotions are perceived and expressed in fiction. Recognizing these influences can add depth to your InnerNex analysis.

"Amina gracefully lowered her gaze when the elder entered the room."

In certain cultures, this gesture might signify respect, humility, or deference, while in others, it might indicate shyness or discomfort.

4. The Unspoken Emotions

Often, what's not being said, or the actions that are subtly described, can hint at underlying emotions. For instance:

"Liam hesitated before handing over the letter."

Here, even though the emotion isn't directly expressed, one might infer anxiety, uncertainty, or apprehension.

5. Interplay of Multiple Emotions

Complex fictional scenarios can evoke a mix of emotions, which can overlap, contrast, or evolve over a short span.

"Claire watched the kids play, laughing heartily, a tear rolling down her cheek."

This scenario indicates joy from the laughter, but the tear suggests there might be elements of nostalgia, melancholy, or perhaps gratitude. The world of fiction is a treasure trove of emotional exploration; dive deep and relish the journey.

CH. 29 ADDING ANOTHER ANGLE:

1. The Overdramatic InnerNex

Imagine amplifying every emotion in a text by ten times!

"She felt a tinge of annoyance when her brother borrowed her book without asking."

"She was utterly devastated, the world coming apart at the seams, all because her treacherous brother dared to pilfer her cherished tome!"

2. InnerNex Role Reversal

Consider a scenario where you swap the emotions of characters.

"As the lion roared, the mouse trembled in fear."

"As the lion whimpered, the mouse stood tall with an air of smug satisfaction."

3. InnerNex in Unexpected Places

Ever tried applying InnerNex to inanimate objects?

"The lonely sock wondered where its partner had vanished in the vast abyss of the washing machine."

4. The Emotion Mixer

Mix and match emotions to create comically unexpected scenarios.

"Excitedly terrified, Bob approached the haunted house that was festooned with neon disco lights."

5. InnerNex Time Machine

Imagine how characters from the past would react to modern-day situations.

"Juliet was in a state of extreme perplexity as she tried to decipher the meaning of a winking emoji sent by Romeo."

CH. 30 APPLYING INNERNEX IN DAILY LIFE:

Understanding fictional emotions is a stepping stone to applying the InnerNex concept in your daily life. Here's how you can utilize the techniques and insights gained from this guide to enhance real-world interactions.

1. Self-awareness in Emotion Recognition:

Every day, take a few moments to self-reflect. Consider your emotional state and the factors influencing it. Are you feeling happy because you accomplished something at work? Or are you feeling down due to a personal setback? Recognizing your own emotions is the first step towards understanding the emotions of others.

Maintain a journal. At the end of each day, note down the dominant emotion you felt and the reason behind it. Over time, you'll start recognizing patterns in your emotional responses.

2. Enhancing Communication:

When conversing with someone, actively listen and watch for emotional cues. Remember, non-verbal cues like facial expressions, body language, and tone of voice often reveal more than words.

During a conversation, try to note down the emotional cues you picked up from the other person. After the conversation, reflect on these cues and assess whether your understanding matched the emotion the person was trying to convey.

3. Building Empathy:

Empathy is the ability to understand and share the feelings of another. By practicing InnerNex in fictional scenarios, you can develop a deeper level of empathy in real-life situations.

The next time someone shares a personal story with you, instead of immediately responding, take a moment to mentally place yourself in their shoes. Feel their emotions, and then respond with understanding.

4. Resolving Conflicts:

Conflicts often arise from misinterpreted emotions. Using the InnerNex technique, try to understand the root emotion causing the conflict. Once you identify it, addressing and resolving the conflict becomes easier.

Reflect on a past conflict. Could identifying the underlying emotion have led to a quicker resolution? How would you approach a similar situation in the future using InnerNex?

5. Personal Growth and Relationships:

By recognizing and understanding emotions, you can navigate relationships more effectively, ensuring mutual respect and understanding.

Think of a relationship (romantic, familial, or friendship) that is important to you. Identify a moment where emotions ran high. Using InnerNex, break down the situation and the emotions involved. Could the outcome have been different with better emotional understanding?

Applying InnerNex in daily life not only enriches personal interactions but also contributes to emotional well-being.

CH. 31 INNERNEX IN POP CULTURE:

The universality of emotions means they're a staple in our entertainment and media. From movies to music, emotions drive stories, character arcs, and even melodies. Let's explore the presence and analysis of these emotions in popular culture.

1. Movies and TV Shows:

Emotions play a pivotal role in storytelling. Think about the last movie or series you watched. The climaxes, the tension, the relief, the humor – all are centered around emotions.

Consider the movie "Inside Out." Not only does it vividly depict emotions as characters, but it also provides a visual representation of how emotions guide our actions, memories, and personal growth.

After watching a movie or episode, take a moment to analyze the main character's emotional journey. What were the significant emotional turning points? How did the emotions drive the story forward?

2. Music:

Lyrics often convey strong emotions, but so do melodies, rhythms, and harmonies. Emotions in music can evoke memories, feelings, and even physiological responses.

The song "Someone Like You" by Adele captures the raw emotion of heartbreak. The lyrics, combined with the melody, touch listeners deeply, often evoking personal memories and feelings.

The next time you listen to your favorite song, try to dissect the emotions it portrays. Is it the lyrics that tug at your heartstrings? Or is it the music itself?

3. Literature:

Books provide a deep dive into a character's psyche. We often get a direct view of a character's thoughts, making it a ripe field for InnerNex application.

In "Pride and Prejudice" by Jane Austen, Elizabeth Bennet's emotions, ranging from disdain, prejudice, love, to self-realization, shape the storyline.

After reading a chapter or book, outline the emotional journey of the main character. How did their emotions dictate their decisions?

4. Video Games:

Modern video games have complex storylines and character developments, often rivaling movies and series in emotional depth.

In the game "The Last of Us," players are taken through a roller-coaster of emotions, from desperation and fear to love and sacrifice.

CH. 32 UTILIZING INNERNEX IN BOOK CLUBS AND STUDY GROUPS:

Book clubs and study groups provide a dynamic platform where diverse opinions and interpretations converge. Implementing InnerNex can revolutionize these discussions by adding a structured approach to analyzing emotions in texts. Let's explore how.

1. In-depth Character Analysis

By using InnerNex, members can dissect the emotions of characters in intricate detail, discussing not just the apparent emotions but also the underlying, more nuanced feelings.

When discussing a character's actions in a specific scene, to pinpoint the exact emotions driving the character, fostering a richer and more insightful discussion.

2. Enhancing Group Dynamics

Cultivating empathy and understanding within the group. Learn to perceive emotions in a detailed manner, better interpersonal dynamics within the group.

Members might disagree on a character's motivations. Using InnerNex, they can analyze the text together, potentially finding a common ground or at least understanding differing viewpoints more clearly.

3. Developing Critical Thinking

The structured approach of InnerNex encourages members to think critically, delving deeper into the narrative and possibly uncovering layers of the story that might not be apparent at first glance.

During a discussion, members might come across a subtle hint of foreshadowing in a character's emotional expression, offering a new perspective on the unfolding events.

4. Collaborative Learning

Collaboratively learn and grow, sharing insights and learning from each other's analyses, which can be a rewarding experience.

Together creating an emotion map for the entire narrative, a visual representation that showcases the emotional journey of the characters throughout the story.

CH. 33 CLOSING THOUGHTS AND FURTHER EXPLORATION:

Having ventured deep into the heart of emotions and their representation in fictional scenarios. Emotions, with their profound depth and diverse spectrum, give life to narratives, making them relatable, powerful, and transformative.

Should this book resonate with readers, I'd love to see your feedback. All reviews, both glowing and constructive, are deeply valued. If the collective passion reaches a milestone of 500 positive reviews — quite an achievement, especially since this is my second book but feels like a first in many ways — it will pave the way for more. ❤❤

(500) Glossary of Emotion Terms

(50000) Online InnerNex Communities, Forums, and Social Media (aesuvious@protonmail.com)

(500) Printable worksheets containing fictional scenarios designed specifically for InnerNex practice. These can be used individually or in group settings for discussions and workshops

The landscape of emotions is vast, and the beauty of it lies in its endless scope for exploration. I hope that these avenues help you toward thriving in your literary endeavors.

You have the potential to tap into the emotional subtext of narratives, giving you insights that go beyond the text. To enrich your every reading experience, deepen your discussions about stories, and provide a foundation for personal growth.

Emotions are universal. They cross boundaries, cultures, and eras. By understanding them in one context, we can better understand them in others.

Remember: every story carries an emotional truth, tucked beneath each person's tree, waiting to be opened. Each real-life scenario also offers an opportunity to apply what you've learned.

Happy learning!